GUESS THE
VERDICT

GUESS THE VERDICT:

Over 100 clever courtroom quizzes to test your legal smarts

HELAINE HUDSON, ESQ.

STERLING PUBLISHING CO., INC.
NEW YORK

Library of Congress Cataloging-in-Publication Data

Hudson, Helaine.
Guess the verdict : Over 100 clever courtroom quizzes to test your
legal smarts / Helaine Hudson.
p. cm.
Includes index.
ISBN 1-4027-1096-8
1. Judgments--United States--Problems, exercises, etc. 2. Verdicts--
United States--Problems, exercises, etc. 3. Judgments--United States--Popular
works. 4. Verdicts--United States--Popular works. I. Title.
KF8990.Z9H83 2004
347.73'77--dc22
2004010746

2   4   6   8   10   9   7   5   3

Published by Sterling Publishing Co., Inc.
387 Park Avenue South, New York, NY 10016
© 2004 by Helaine Hudson
Distributed in Canada by Sterling Publishing
ᶜ/o Canadian Manda Group, 165 Dufferin Street,
Toronto, Ontario, Canada M6K 3H6
Distributed in Great Britain by Chrysalis Books Group PLC
The Chrysalis Building, Bramley Road, London W10 6SP, England
Distributed in Australia by Capricorn Link (Australia) Pty. Ltd.
P.O. Box 704, Windsor, NSW 2756, Australia

Sterling ISBN 1-4027-1096-8

For information about custom editions, special sales, premium and
corporate purchases, please contact Sterling Special Sales
Department at 800-805-5489 or specialsales@sterlingpub.com.

Contents

Introduction

If you've picked up this book, you likely have an interest in law—either you are a student or an attorney seeking to test your know-how—or you just like mind games.

Guess the Verdict is filled with real cases that were heard in the United States. (The parties' names have been changed to make the reading more fun and the guessing more difficult.) The cases were selected not only for their often funny or intriguing facts, or their significance in establishing precedent or representing the most common rules of law in our society, but because they challenge our instincts and gut feelings—they could go either way and still be "right." For this reason, many of the cases were appealed and reversed. Other cases are included because they involve unusual questions (for example, are your blood and tissue samples considered your property?) or because the subject matter is of contemporary interest, such as in the fields of technology and entertainment.

The cases were also selected and organized so that the reader who has not been to law school will get a feel for the typical three-year law-school curriculum in the United States. First, the cases are organized into two sections—one for each of the "first-year" subjects (Contracts, Torts, Criminal Law, Property, and Constitutional Law), and one for "electives" taken in years two and three (such as Intellectual Property and Wills and Estates). Then, the cases are "briefed"; that is, the *facts* of each case and the *issue* are presented to the court. The court's decision (answer) for each case is in the Holdings chapter, along with a brief explanation of the court's rationale and the general rule of law upheld in each case. The name and formal legal citation of each case are also in the Holdings chapter.

For those of you who have been to law school, perhaps this setup will make you nostalgic. You might even recognize some of the cases—there are a few "landmarks" included, which should be no-brainers for attorneys and legal buffs. For those who are in their early courtship with courtroom curiosity, these will be more challenging. As for the rest of the cases, regardless of who you are and how much you think you know, you will feel tested, probably learn some law, and, most of all, have a good time in the process.

While I was writing this book, my husband, an Englishman, served as judge to see if the cases were interesting and challenging enough to be included (and to prove to me how smart he is if he correctly guessed the verdict; or, if he guessed incorrectly, how United States law is unruly and unfair). He did well overall, but I had to remind him of some basic guidelines for playing with this book: First, don't add any facts—you need only the information cited to decide the case. Second, when playing with others (see the last chapter to learn how to do this), the game will go more smoothly if you answer the question with a yes or a no—remember the game is simply Guess the Verdict. You can (and no doubt will) analyze and discuss the cases later, after you check the answers. The best way is to go with your initial instinct, apply some reason, and then make an educated guess as to the verdict.

Finally, you will have to give up any notion that rules of law, once you know them, are easy to apply. Outcomes depend on facts. They may also depend on the wording of a statute or prior cases. So if you think that one case seems like another, you might want to think again. This is not to say that the law is random or inconsistent. If you reread the facts (or consider the statute or prior cases), you might find important distinctions or guidelines on which courts have based their decisions. These verdicts have created a richer, more robust body of law consisting of interrelated rules that take into account real (albeit often strange) situations.

Enjoy this book on your own or play with friends (or adversaries). And remember: If the law is on your side, pound the law. If the facts are on your side, pound the facts. And if you've got neither, pound the table!

–Helaine Hudson

About the Author

Helaine Hudson is a practicing corporate attorney in the New York City area. Formerly known as Helaine Fine, she graduated *magna cum laude* from Brooklyn Law School, where she was an articles editor for the *Brooklyn Journal of International Law* and a member of the Moot Court Honor Society. Helaine lives in Westchester, New York with her husband, Tim.

GUESS THE
VERDICT

First Year

CRIMINAL LAW

1. Best Laid Plans

Facts: Bob, Bill, and Marty made a detailed plan about how to rob a bank. They loaded up a car with guns, covered the license plate, and drove to the bank. They didn't rob it because there were too many people around. Meanwhile, one of their friends ratted them out to the police. The next week, they went again to do the job with guns and a covered license plate. When they arrived, there were cops around, so they kept on driving and didn't rob the bank.

Issue: Are Bob, Bill, and Marty guilty of attempted robbery?
Holding: page 88

2. Vain Attempt

Facts: David and Berdy wanted to kill Berdy's husband, Ed, to collect insurance money. David met Dylan through a friend and hired him to kill Ed for $600. David was unaware that Dylan was a police officer. David and Dylan met a few times and planned that Dylan would go to Ed and Berdy's house, kill Ed, and fake a robbery. When Dylan arrived at Ed and Berdy's house, he arrested David.

Issue: Is David guilty of attempted murder?
Holding: page 88

3. Take the Money and Run

Facts: Cheeky Courier Corp. had a contract with Big Bucks Bank to pick up and count Big Bucks' deposits and deliver them within 72 hours. Since Cheeky was able to count the money in 24 hours, it used the remaining 48 hours to earn interest on the money at another bank. Cheeky always delivered the money to Big Bucks, but kept the interest earned.

Issue: Is Cheeky guilty of larceny?
Holding: page 88

4. Ex Post Facto

Facts: Albert led a demonstration on a navy base after he had been legally banned from the premises. The government charged Albert for violation of the ban under a specific law, and he was convicted. Albert's conviction was overturned because Albert had a First Amendment right to demonstrate. The government appealed to the United States Supreme Court, and, before the case was decided, Albert demonstrated again on the base. Then, the Supreme Court held that Albert's First Amendment right was not protected because Albert had demonstrated in defiance of a valid order banning him from the premises.

Issue: Is Albert guilty of violating the ban for the second demonstration?

Holding: page 89

5. Drunk Again

Facts: Bill was an alcoholic and had an irresistible compulsion to drink. One day he was arrested by the police for being drunk out in public view. Nobody forced him to be there—he went of his own volition.

Issues: A: Is Bill's alcoholism a defense to public drunkenness? B: Is it "cruel and unusual" to punish him because of his illness, thereby violating the Eighth Amendment?

Holding: page 89

6. Russian Roulette

Facts: Two friends, Billy and Malcolm, were hanging around one day in a deli when Malcolm showed Billy a gun he had taken from his uncle. Malcolm loaded the gun. He then suggested to Billy that they play a game of Russian roulette. Billy agreed, and Malcolm put the gun up to Billy's head and pulled the trigger three times. The third shot killed Billy.

Issue: Is Malcolm guilty of intentional murder?

Holding: page 89

7. Possession Is Nine-Tenths of the Law

Facts: Bill and Linda signed a contract to sell their house to Liz and Matt, excluding personal property and including fixtures, plumbing, shrubs, and window treatments. When the sale closed and Liz and

Matt moved in, certain items were missing, such as an unattached washstand and commode and several fruit trees. These were found by the lower court to have been either included in the sale or covered by a separate agreement and should have been left in the house by Bill and Linda.

Issue: Are Bill and Linda guilty of larceny?
Holding: page 90

8. Self-Defense

Facts: Charlie went to Benny's house to steal some car parts. While Charlie was in the act, Benny came out of his house and told Charlie to stop. Benny then got his gun. When he went back outside, Charlie was in his own car ready to leave. Benny then threatened to shoot Charlie. Charlie got out of his car, grabbed a lug wrench, and came toward Benny with it, threatening Benny. Benny pointed the gun at Charlie and told him not to come any further or he'd shoot him. When Charlie continued, Benny shot him and Charlie died.

Issue: Can Benny claim self-defense?
Holding: page 90

9. Vicarious Kill

Facts: Larry, Bert, and Bob went to rob a liquor store. Larry sat in the getaway car while Bert and Bob went into the store to rob it. Bert pointed a gun at the store owner while Bob chattered insanely, threatened to kill the owner, and ordered him to put money in a bag. The store owner's wife fired a shot at Bert, starting a gunfight. The store owner eventually shot Bob and Bert in self-defense, injuring Bert and killing Bob.

Issue: Is Larry guilty for the murder of Bob?
Holding: page 90

10. Drunk and Disorderly

Facts: The cops arrested a drunken Mickey in his home and then drove him to the highway, and took him out of the police car. He started acting drunk, yelling and swearing loudly out on the highway.

Issue: Is Mickey guilty of public drunkenness?
Holding: page 91

11. Scared to Death

Facts: Terry broke into Mark's office to commit robbery at gunpoint. Terry ordered Mark, who was sixty years old and had a bad heart, to lie on the floor along with other employees while he took money and made his escape. During the robbery, Mark's chest began pounding. Within a few minutes after Terry left, Mark felt chest pains. He then collapsed and died of a heart attack. The medical experts confirmed that an extreme event would have had to precipitate the attack.

Issue: Is Terry guilty of murder?
Holding: page 91

12. The Drunkard's Defense

Facts: Alan, who had been drinking, was acting drunk and disorderly in public. The police tried to arrest him, and Alan resisted. He eventually grabbed an officer's gun and shot the officer in the leg. Alan was charged with assault with intent to murder, but he claimed that because he was drunk he was unable to form the intent to kill.

Issue: Does Alan have a valid defense?
Holding: page 91

13. Cruise Control

Facts: Joe was driving his car on a highway where the speed limit was fifty-five miles per hour. He placed the car in "cruise control" mode at fifty-five, but it stuck in the "accelerate" position. He tried to disengage the cruise control and to brake to slow down, with no success. The car sped up to seventy-five miles per hour. Joe later had to have the defective cruise control repaired. However, he was arrested for speeding.

Issue: Does Joe have a valid defense for speeding?
Holding: page 92

14. Depraved Heart

Facts: One afternoon, Ian got drunk and went for a drive. Witnesses observed him at various times driving between seventy and one hundred miles per hour in forty-five miles per hour zones. He was also seen driving southbound in the northbound lanes to avoid traffic. Eventually, Ian lost control of his car, sliding across a highway and striking Halley's car. Halley died almost immediately from severe injuries.

Issues: A: Is Ian guilty of murder? B: Is Ian guilty of manslaughter (reckless homicide)?
Holding: page 92

15. Duty to Save

Facts: James was married, but was a bit of a cad and ran around with women other than his wife. One night while his wife was out of town, he took Blanche to his apartment. Blanche took excessive amounts of drugs and became sick. James didn't get medical attention for her. A neighbor eventually called an ambulance, but it was too late and Blanche died of an overdose.

Issue: Is James guilty of manslaughter?
Holding: page 93

16. Just Hanging Around

Facts: Bart, being bored and having no social life, went to a house with the intention to burglarize it. Val, Bart's friend, went with Bart to the house, planning to help. Instead, he stood outside and watched Bart do it. Val didn't help in any way. When Bart was done, they both fled the scene and were arrested.

Issue: Is Val guilty as an accomplice?
Holding: page 93

17. Time of Death

Facts: Rose was driving and accidentally hit Milt because he was walking in an intersection. Rose stopped momentarily after impact, Milt's body rolled off the car, and Rose kept driving. She eventually abandoned her car about 200 yards from the scene and later reported the car stolen. Milt was found dead, wedged under Rose's car. At trial, the medical evidence was unclear as to whether Milt had died on impact or some time after Rose left the scene.

Issue: Is Rose guilty of manslaughter?
Holding: page 93

18. Audacious Auditor

Facts: Zeb worked for the IRS and had access to confidential computer files, including personal information of United States citizens. Zeb was not authorized to access many of these files, but he did so anyway. He did not use the information obtained from the files; he only accessed and read the files of people he knew.

Issue: Is Zeb guilty of computer fraud?
Holding: page 93

19. Sharp Shopper

Facts: Matthew was "shopping" for clothes in Jerry's Department Store. He took a shirt from the men's department and brought it to the ladies' department, where he told the clerk that he had bought it and wanted to return it for a refund. He didn't have a receipt, so he was only able to get a store credit. After the transaction was completed, a store detective, who saw the whole thing, detained Matthew.

Issue: Is Matthew guilty of larceny?
Holding: page 94

20. Legal Fees?

Facts: Graham, an attorney, represented Frank, who had been arrested and charged with disorderly conduct. Frank, whose English wasn't very good, was seeking United States citizenship and was afraid that the arrest would affect his status. Graham said he wasn't sure what he could do about the situation, but that he would speak to the arresting officer. Graham told Frank that his fee would be $200, but that Frank would have to give him an additional $2,000 "for the police." Frank gave a total of $2,200 to Graham. The police officer spoke to Graham and then told Frank he was not in any trouble. Graham never gave any money to the officer and kept it all for himself.

Issue: Is Graham guilty of theft by false pretense?
Holding: page 94

21. Wildfire

Facts: Artie intentionally set fire to a couch in his fifth floor apartment. The fire spread to other parts of the fifth and sixth floors. An unrelated fire broke out on the second floor, which created a dense smoke. As firefighters tried to control the fifth floor fire, they were enveloped by smoke from the second floor fire. Firefighter Mark couldn't get out and he died. There was no evidence that Artie had started the fire on the second floor.

Issue: Is Artie guilty of reckless murder?
Holding: page 94

22. Money Bags

Facts: Jim worked for an armored car service. He collected bags of money that belonged to various banks and delivered them to the banks. Occasionally, Jim would skim money from the bags and keep it.

Issue: Is Jim guilty of larceny?
Holding: page 95

23. False Pretenses

Facts: Andy was broke. His bank account was closed, but he still had an ATM card. He used the card at an ATM machine at a ShopGood store and withdrew $19,000. ShopGood checked cards electronically through another bank that would approve or disapprove the transaction through its own electronic system. The bank approved the transaction.

Issue: Is Andy guilty of theft by false pretense?
Holding: page 95

CONTRACTS

24. This Land Is My Land

Facts: On Monday, Joel offered in writing to sell Adele his land. The offer stated it would remain open until Friday. But on Thursday, Adele heard from Tim that Joel was offering the land to Sylvia. So Adele rushed a letter of acceptance over to Joel's house and left it with his mother, who forgot to give him the letter. On Friday, Adele's attorney saw Joel and gave him a copy of the acceptance letter, but Joel said it was too late, he had already sold the land to Sylvia.

Issue: Is Adele entitled to compel Joel to transfer the property to her?

Holding: page 95

25. Just Reward

Facts: Bernie was murdered on June 5. On June 6, a private group placed an ad offering a reward for anyone furnishing information leading to the arrest of the murderer. The police suspected Clyde. On June 11, they questioned Mary, the mother of Clyde's girlfriend. Mary informed the police of exactly where Clyde was. Mary then saw the offer for the reward in the paper on June 12. Clyde was arrested. Mary sought the reward.

Issue: Is Mary entitled to the reward?
Holding: page 95

26. Family Values

Facts: Old Bill promised to give his nephew, Willy, $5,000 if Willy refrained from drinking, smoking, gambling, and swearing until his twenty-first birthday. Willy agreed, and lived up to his promise. Old Bill continued to hold the money for Willy so he wouldn't squander it. When Old Bill died, Harriet, to whom Willy had assigned his right to the money, sought to get the money from Old Bill's estate.

Issue: Was there a valid contract between Old Bill and Willy? (Note: Whether the contract was oral or in writing does not affect the outcome of this case.)
Holding: page 96

27. Minor Infraction

Facts: When she turned 16, Sophie went with her aunt to buy her first car from Bob. After a week, Sophie discovered that the car needed major repairs, so she brought it back to Bob. Sophie couldn't afford to pay for the repairs, so she decided to cancel the contract and told Bob to return her money.

Issue: Does Bob have to return Sophie's money?
Holding: page 96

28. What's Wrong With This Picture?

Facts: Shelby Brooks, a famous actress, had been acting and modeling since she was a young girl. When Shelby was about ten years old, her mother gave written consent to a photographer to take photos of Shelby posing nude. At the time, Shelby did not object. The negatives, of course, were the property of the photographer. When Shelby was about 17, she wasn't happy that these photographs were being made public in various ways, and sought to buy the negatives from the photographer. When he refused to sell them to her, she sought in court to stop him from using the photos.

Issue: Does the consent made by her mother on Shelby's behalf continue to bind Shelby?

Holding: page 96

29. Dominion and Control

Facts: Rebecca gave Tony money to hold. Tony gave Rebecca a paper that had several columns, one of which contained numbers totaling the amount Rebecca gave to Tony. The paper was dated, but there was no other writing on it. Rebecca gave Sarah the paper, intending to give Sarah the money that Tony held. Tony didn't know of this. Rebecca died, and Sarah tried to get the money, as opposed to Rebecca's heirs.

Issue: Did Rebecca make a valid assignment of the money to Sarah?
Holding: page 96

30. Promises, Promises

Facts: David, Marion's adult son, became very ill while returning from a long trip. He couldn't make it home, so Henry, a stranger, took David in and nursed him until he eventually died. Marion wrote a letter to Henry promising to pay all of Henry's expenses for caring for David, but she later refused to pay.

Issue: Does Marion have to pay Henry?
Holding: page 97

31. Do IOU?

Facts: Taylor broke into Henry's house to attack Liz, who had run there for protection. Liz grabbed an axe and was about to cut Taylor's head open, when Henry grabbed the axe and saved Taylor's life. Henry suffered a serious injury to his hand from the axe. Taylor, grateful to Henry, promised to pay Henry's medical expenses. Taylor made a few payments and then stopped. Taylor sued Henry for breach of contract.

Issue: Do Taylor and Henry have a valid contract?
Holding: page 97

32. You Dance Divinely

Facts: Ginger, a 51-year-old widow, had always wanted to take dance lessons. She was encouraged by Gene, who worked for Fred's Dance School, to attend a dance party at the school. At the party, Gene emphatically shared his opinions with Ginger regarding her innate dance talent and potential to be an excellent dancer. Over 16 months, Ginger purchased, through Gene's sales promotions, over 2,000 hours of lessons at Fred's for an outlay of $31,000, always pursuant to a signed contract. Gene continued to barrage Ginger with his compliments and opinions about her wonderful dancing, and often sold her additional lessons while she still had over 1,000 hours of unused lessons. Actually, Ginger had no ability, and Gene knew it.

Issue: Did Fred's fraudulently induce Ginger to enter into the contracts?
Holding: page 97

33. Oops!

Facts: While hunting wolves, Elmer mistakenly shot Timmy's dog because of the dog's striking resemblance to a wolf. The dog died.

Issue: Is Elmer liable to Timmy for damages for killing the dog?

Holding: page 98

34. Trespasser Traps

Facts: Keith owned a country house that he did not live in regularly. Keith posted "no trespassing" signs on the property. Over the years, there were a series of break-ins, so Keith rigged up a shotgun to one of the bedroom doors which was designed to shoot an intruder in the legs upon entering the room. Paula entered the house one day to steal some antiques. When she entered the bedroom, the gun went off, shot her in the leg, and seriously and permanently deformed her.

Issue: Is Keith allowed to protect his property this way?
Holding: page 98

35. What a Buzz

Facts: Robin went to visit Missy, who lived in an apartment building. When she arrived, Robin rang Missy from the intercom in the outer lobby. Missy tried to let Robin in by using the electric buzzer to release the door lock. The buzzer failed, and while Missy was going to the lobby to let Robin in, Robin was attacked by a stranger and injured. Robin sued Missy's landlord for negligence for having the broken buzzer.

Issue: Is the landlord negligent?
Holding: page 98

36. Just Blowing Smoke

Facts: Lenny was an antismoking spokesperson. He went on Conrad's radio show to discuss the dangers of smoking. Conrad encouraged Fred, another station employee, to blow smoke in Lenny's face during the show to annoy and humiliate him.

Issue: Did Fred commit battery?
Holding: page 98

37. Pole Fault

Facts: Ron and Barry were driving, and their vehicles collided. Ron lost control and smashed into a utility pole owned and maintained by Eddie's Electric Company. The pole fell on impact and seriously injured Bernie. The pole was not designed to resist being knocked down.

Issue: Is Eddie's Electric Company liable for injuries to Bernie?
Holding: page 99

38. Emotional Distress

Facts: Little John was hit by a car driven by Margot. Little John's sister ran to tell Barbara, their mom, who was nearby but had not seen or heard the accident. When Barbara arrived at the scene, she saw Little John unconscious and covered with blood, and she had a serious emotional reaction.

Issue: Is Margot liable to Barbara for inflicting emotional distress?
Holding: page 99

39. Proximate Cause

Facts: Roy was riding a city bus to work. Instead of pulling over to the curb as required by law, the bus stopped in a center traffic lane to let people off. At the same time, a truck smashed into the back of the bus when the truck's brakes failed. Roy was injured and sued both the owner of the bus and the owner of the truck.

Issues: A: Was the owner of the bus negligent because the driver did not obey the traffic laws? B: Was the owner of the truck negligent because of the brake failure?
Holding: page 99

40. Do I Do?

Facts: Chris was a psychiatric patient of Dr. Do-Nothing at a college psychiatric hospital. During their sessions, Chris told Dr. Do-Nothing that he intended to kill Nicole because she rejected his advances. Dr. Do-Nothing informed campus police and other psychiatrists of the situation, and they all decided that Chris did not need to be confined. Nobody told Nicole about this. Chris stopped going to treatment. Two months later, he shot and killed Nicole.

Issue: Was Dr. Do-Nothing negligent?
Holding: page 100

41. Please Release Me

Facts: Bob and Carol sued Dom in civil court for gross negligence in the death of Bob and Carol's son, who was killed when the car Dom was driving struck the boy. Dom sued Carco for its share of any damages to be paid to Bob and Carol based on a defect in the car that had interfered with proper brake function during the incident. Unknown to Dom, Carco paid Bob and Carol a reasonable settlement amount in exchange for a release of any claims they had against Carco.

Issue: Can Carco have any further liability to Dom or to Bob and Carol?
Holding: page 100

42. Public or Private?

Facts: Stan and Oliver, Senator Dud's former employees, sneaked into the Senator's office and removed documents. They copied the documents, returned the originals, and gave the copies to Realvu Publishers, who, knowing they had been improperly taken, and using information from the documents, published several articles about Dud's career and possible improper activities.

Issue: Is Realvu liable for invasion of privacy?
Holding: page 100

43. Private Parts

Facts: Joanne, a private individual, was abducted at gunpoint by her estranged husband and taken to their old apartment. He then forced her to disrobe so she couldn't escape. The police eventually rescued her, but had to rush her out to protect her from harm. She had no time to get dressed, so when she emerged from the apartment she only had a dish towel to cover herself with. While the event was happening, a local newspaper was on the scene and obtained pictures of Joanne's rescue. In connection with the story, the paper published photos of Joanne nude except for the dish towel.

Issue: Is the paper liable for invasion of privacy?
Holding: page 101

44. A Shot in the Dark

Facts: Mark, Gene, and Tom were out hunting. Suddenly a quail flew by in the direction of Tom. Mark and Gene both negligently shot their guns in that direction, and Tom was hit in the eye by a bullet. The evidence couldn't show which gun actually shot Tom.

Issue: Are Mark and Gene both liable to Tom for damages?
Holding: page 101

45. Spam

Facts: Spamco sent unsolicited e-mail advertisements to subscribers of Connectco, a large Internet service provider. Connectco requested that Spamco stop doing this. Spamco continued and increased the amount of spam being sent to Connectco's subscribers, many of whom closed their accounts.

Issue: Has Spamco committed a trespass?
Holding: page 101

46. Flight from Reality

Facts: Amelia was in a bad car accident. She drove onto the wrong side of the road and, when she saw an oncoming car (driven by Charles), she stepped on the gas and crashed into it, causing Charles injuries. She told a psychiatrist, whose testimony was credible, that she suddenly believed God was driving, and she had hit the gas because she was sure she could fly and that the car would become airborne. This had never happened to Amelia before.

Issue: Is Amelia relieved of liability for negligence?
Holding: page 102

47. What a Drag

Facts: Norm and Jeff had fast cars and decided to drag race. During the race, Norm was driving in the wrong lane and, when they went over a hill, Norm's car hit Larry's oncoming car. Jeff's car never hit Larry's.

Issue: Is Jeff liable to Larry for damages?
Holding: page 102

48. To Be or Not to Be

Facts: For several months after Dr. Bob was in a car accident with another driver, he suffered serious head injuries, brain damage, and seizures. It was determined that the impact from the accident caused Dr. Bob's injuries. The injuries were so severe that Dr. Bob could no longer work, and his personal life became difficult. In addition, Dr. Bob's mother was diagnosed with cancer and his wife was already suffering from paralysis from an unrelated incident. Dr. Bob eventually killed himself about seven months after the accident; on the day of his suicide, he had three seizures and was very disoriented. He had previously bought a gun, and left suicide notes for his family indicating that he knew what he was doing.

Issue: Assuming the other driver was negligent, can the other driver be liable to Dr. Bob's family for the death of Dr. Bob by suicide?
Holding: page 102

49. Hands Off

Facts: Rupert delivered newspapers for a living. He worked for a newspaper distribution company that distributed several newspapers, including those published by Okay Publishing. Rupert had no direct relationship or contact with Okay Publishing, but had to adhere to some of their standards such as time of delivery, territory, and securing the papers with rubber bands. One day Rupert, feeling a bit hostile, broke Mary's screen door while delivering a newspaper and then, after an argument ensued, hit Mary, causing an injury.

Issue: Is Okay Publishing liable for Rupert's negligence?
Holding: page 103

50. Party Animals

Facts: Rick attended a party hosted by some of his college classmates, who were all under the legal age for drinking. The hosts regularly threw parties, and sometimes charged admission because they supplied the booze. Rick, who was also under the legal age to drink, got drunk at one of the parties and was struck by a car while walking home that night.

Issue: Are Rick's classmates liable to Rick for negligently serving him alcohol?
Holding: page 103

51. Last Call

Facts: A group of minors were out drinking at the Whirlybird cafe. The Whirlybird did not check IDs. One of the minors, while driving home drunk, struck another vehicle, injuring Bridget.

Issue: Is the Whirlybird liable to Bridget?
Holding: page 103

52. Blood on the Tracks

Facts: Manuel was strolling along some railroad tracks owned by the Fast Track Railroad Company. He was not at a public crossing. Manuel's foot got stuck in the track and he couldn't get it out. Meanwhile, the driver of the oncoming train did not see Manuel until he was practically on him, and he couldn't stop in time. The train ran over Manuel's foot and injured it.

Issue: Is Fast Track liable to Manuel?
Holding: page 104

CONSTITUTIONAL LAW

53. Public Figure

Facts: The *Tell Truth Times* ran an ad describing racial problems taking place in a United States city. The ad accused the police of violence and generally attributed misconduct to the police. Sully, the Chief of Police, sued the *Times* for libel. The trial court found that the statements in the ad had been damaging to Sully's reputation. The *Times* could not prove that everything stated in the ad was completely true because of some inaccuracies.

Issue: Is The Tell Truth Times *liable for libel?*
Holding: page 104

54. Fair Trial

Facts: The defense counsel in Jeffrey's murder trial requested that the judge close the trial to the public, including reporters, to prevent the jury from being influenced by witnesses and onlookers during court recesses. The prosecution agreed, and the trial was closed. However, there had been no evidence presented to or considered by the judge indicating that public knowledge and sentiment would interfere with the jury's ability to be fair.

Issue: Did the court improperly interfere with the rights of a free press?
Holding: page 105

55. What Is a Taking?

Facts: Apples were a primary cash crop in Virginia. Unfortunately, many apple orchards in Virginia were being destroyed by a disease carried by cedar trees. Virginia enacted a law ordering all property owners to destroy any cedar trees on their property. No payment was made to any property owners for the loss of value to their property due to removal of the cedar trees.

Issue: Does Virginia have to pay the property owners for cutting down the trees?
Holding: page 105

56. I Know It When I See It

Facts: Steamy Theater advertised "adult" films on posters at the theater. The films (not the posters) contained nudity and sex acts. Steamy had signs put up stating that only persons over 21 with valid identification would be allowed in to see the films. Steamy also posted warning signs stating that anyone who might be offended by nudity should not see the films. Nonetheless, the city prosecuted Steamy for violating its obscenity laws.

Issue: Can Steamy be guilty of obscenity charges if the films were shown to consenting adults only?
Holding: page 105

57. Immediate Lawless Action

Facts: Mr. Lily, leader of a violent racist organization, made a speech to a group of his followers while they stood around a burning cross. Some of the men had guns. Lily made nasty racist remarks and stated, "if the government continues to suppress whites, there might have to be some revenge taken." Lily was arrested for violating a statute that prohibited advocacy of violence as a means of accomplishing reform.

Issue: Is Mr. Lily's speech protected under the First Amendment?
Holding: page 105

58. Alien Rights

Facts: Anna, Anita, and Alberto were not allowed to attend public school in Texas because they were from foreign countries and were not living legally in the United States. Texas passed this law because it didn't want to encourage illegal immigrants to come into the United States or the burden of educating children who were unlikely to remain in Texas and contribute to the state.

Issue: Can Texas deny Anna, Anita, and Alberto a public education?
Holding: page 106

59. Double Standard

Facts: Mr. Milquetoast's wife died and he filed for her Social Security benefits, which she had been paying for all the years she worked. The Social Security office said he could get benefits only if his wife had been responsible for half his support while she was alive. Meanwhile, Mrs. Freeride's husband died, and she was entitled to receive full benefits without having to show anything about support from her husband.

Issue: Is the Social Security office's rule constitutional?
Holding: page 106

PROPERTY

60. Losers Weepers

Facts: Heath had a very exciting job as an airplane safety inspector. One day, while servicing a plane, Heath found a package in the wing containing $18,000. The plane was owned by Linda's company. Attempts were made to find the rightful owner, but nobody claimed the money.

Issue: Is Heath entitled to the money?
Holding: page 106

61. Stair Master

Facts: Gretta and Massimo were next-door neighbors. Gretta built a concrete walkway and stairs leading to her front door. Many years later, Massimo found out that a portion of Gretta's stairs was on his property. Gretta didn't know about this until Massimo told her.

Issue: Does Gretta have to remove the stairs?
Holding: page 107

62. The Issue of Tissue

Facts: Roger needed treatment for a serious illness. He had many tests and operations, which included the taking of blood and tissue samples. Roger signed all the necessary papers for his treatments and for removal of the blood and tissue. However, unbeknownst to him, once the tissue was removed, Dr. Noall used it for research. The doctor eventually developed new cells for which a patent was issued.

Issue: Did Dr. Noall improperly use Roger's property?
Holding: page 107

63. Self-Help

Facts: Jordana lived in a building owned by Terry. The lease said that if Jordana didn't pay her rent, Terry had a right of "re-entry" and an interest in Jordana's personal belongings to secure rent payments. Owing to money problems, Jordana didn't pay rent for two months, so, while she wasn't home, Terry unlocked her apartment, took her belongings, put them in storage, and refused to allow Jordana to get back in her apartment.

Issue: Is Terry liable to Jordana for forcible entry and improperly taking her property?
Holding: page 108

64. Quiet Enjoyment

Facts: Jack and Jill lived in a building owned by Olaf. They had a valid lease. Everything was going well until Olaf rented the building next door to a bar, which was very noisy on a regular basis, causing many sleepless nights for Jack and Jill. Olaf warned the bar to quiet down, but it would always become noisy again. Jack and Jill left the apartment permanently before the lease expired.

Issue: A: Did Olaf evict Jack and Jill? B: Are Jack and Jill liable to Olaf for the rent?
Holding: page 108

65. Running with the Land

Facts: Andy and Andrea had a licensed winemaking business on their property. They also had some strange pets—seven llamas. The neighborhood association sued Andy and Andrea, claiming there were restrictions on the land to which all owners had to adhere; these restrictions were recorded in a public office, and prohibited commercial use of the land and having llamas. However, Andy and Andrea's deed of title did not mention these restrictions.

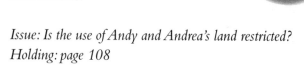

Issue: Is the use of Andy and Andrea's land restricted?
Holding: page 108

Electives

INTELLECTUAL PROPERTY

66. Right of Publicity

Facts: Vanity Brown was a well-known hostess of a popular television game show. She made lots of money selling her likeness to advertisers. Sam's Electronic Corporation published an ad for its video recorders depicting a robot with a hairdo and gown that looked just like Vanity's style. The robot was standing next to a board game that was easily recognized as Vanity's game show. No actual image of Vanity appeared in the ad. Vanity was unhappy because she had never given permission to Sam's to use the robot that way, so she sued Sam's.

Issue: Is Sam's liable for misappropriating Vanity Brown's identity?

Holding: page 109

67. Pig Tale

Facts: Cool Toy Corporation sold a line of very popular stuffed beanbag animals, including Squealer the Pig. Cool Toy held a copyright for Squealer. Three years later, Hot Toy Corporation sold a line of beanbag animals, including Preston the Pig. Preston was practically identical to Squealer, and looked nothing like a real pig or any known fictional pig character.

Hot Toy's designer swore under oath that she had not copied Squealer, and that Preston was an independent creation. There were some differences between design sketches of Preston and Squealer, but those differences did not exist in the final version of Preston.

Issue: Can Cool Toy Corporation stop Hot Toy from selling Preston on the grounds of copyright infringement?
Holding: page 109

68. Great Idea!

Facts: Brian Brain, a movie writer, read a synopsis based on actual events to the secretary of the famous director Willy Bolder. The secretary told Brian that if Bolder used the idea in a film, Brian would be paid. A year later, Bolder produced a film based on the idea.

Issue: Assuming there was a valid contract between Brian and Bolder for payment for the idea, is Brian entitled to payment for an idea?
Holding: page 109

69. Program Protection

Facts: Dr. Buck, a dentist, hired Mr. Hack to design a computer program for dental labs. They agreed that Dr. Buck would receive a percentage of sales made by Hack to other dentists. Hack researched the industry for developing and marketing the program, and he copyrighted the program. Dr. Buck later developed a similar program, using Hack's program.

Issue: Is Dr. Buck liable for infringement of the computer program?
Holding: page 110

70. Trade Secret

Facts: DoWell, a large chemical company, developed a secret process for making a substance that gave it a huge advantage over competitors. DoWell took precautions to protect the secrecy of the process, but Chris, being creative, flew a private plane over a new DoWell plant during construction and took photographs that revealed the process. Chris then sold the photos.

Issue: Did Chris misappropriate DoWell's trade secret?
Holding: page 110

71. Public Display

Facts: Fairview Video operated a business where members of the public could rent a copyrighted film on videotape for viewing in a private room provided by Fairview.

Issue: Does this business infringe on the copyright owner's rights?
Holding: page 110

72. That's My Color!

Facts: Paddy's Manufacturing Company made and sold covers for commercial clothing presses. Paddy's covers were a distinctive greenish-gold. Coverco Manufacturing later started making and selling the same color pads, so Paddy's rushed to the trademark office to register the color and sought to stop Coverco from selling its pads.

Issue: Can Paddy's register the color as a trademark?
Holding: page 111

WILLS AND ESTATES

73. Hanky-Panky

Facts: Hank and Henny were happily married for 40 years. About two years before his death, Hank began accusing Henny of being unfaithful. He regularly expressed this belief to other people, even strangers. Friends and family thought Hank was obsessed with the idea, although he was rational in other respects. Hank, on his own, sought help from a psychiatrist. About a month before his death, Hank left Henny and prepared a new will, leaving to Henny only the minimum amount required by law. The rest of his fortune was left to other family members.

Issue: Can Hank's will be invalidated?
Holding: page 111

74. Virtual Parents

Facts: When Megan was three years old, her mother died. Her father gave her to Peter and Virginia. Peter and Virginia raised Megan until she married, and Megan always used Peter and Virginia's last name. There was no formal adoption agreement between Megan's father and Peter and Virginia, but when Megan was nine, Peter and Virginia told her she was adopted. Peter and Virginia died without wills.

Issue: Is Megan entitled to inherit Peter and Virginia's estate?
Holding: page 111

75. Brotherly Love

Facts: Jacob Sr.'s will said that when he died, his land would be given equally to each of his three sons, Arthur, Erwinn, and Jacob, Jr. After the will was made, Jacob Sr. signed over a deed to Arthur for one-third of the land and to Erwinn for one-third of the land. He wrote a letter to Jacob Jr. asking Jacob Jr. if he wanted his land deeded to him. Before Jacob Jr. had a chance to respond, Jacob Sr. died.

Issue: Are Arthur and Erwinn each entitled to one-third of the land that was left in Jacob Sr.'s estate when he died?
Holding: page 112

76. Hear Ye, Hear Ye

Facts: Connie was very sick and confined to her deathbed in a tiny room. She had a will drawn up by an attorney. She signed it in bed, and the witnesses signed in the next room. Connie could not see the witnesses, but they spoke to Connie during the signing and each immediately went to Connie's bedside and showed her his signature. Connie lived in a state where the law required that for a will to be valid, witnesses had to sign in the presence of the testator.

Issue: Is Connie's will valid?
Holding: page 112

77. The Paper Chase

Facts: Nancy's will left everything to Theo except for specific gifts to other people. The other gifts were listed on a "memorandum" that Nancy had in her possession at the time she made the will. The will referenced the memorandum. After her will was made, Nancy made a note in a notebook leaving an expensive painting to Carl. She later executed two amendments to her will, which, among other things, confirmed the terms of her original will.

Issue: A: Is the memorandum a valid part of Nancy's will?
B: Is Carl entitled to the painting?
Holding: page 112

78. What's in a Name?

Facts: In her will, Johanna left her estate equally to "her nephew Raymond Smith and his wife Mabel Smith." Raymond's current wife was named Evelyn Smith, and Johanna loved her very much. Ray's former wife was Mabel, but her last name was no longer Smith because she had remarried. Mabel thought she should get half the estate, although she had had no contact with Johanna for many years. Other relatives wanted to invalidate the bequest to the wife completely so they could get half the estate.

Issues: A: Is the bequest invalid? B: Is Mabel entitled to half the estate?

Holding: page 112

EVIDENCE

79. What Is Hearsay, Anyway?

Facts: Ms. Reaper slipped and fell in the parking lot of the Grim Funeral Home and sued for damages. At trial, Ms. Reaper's attorney wanted to bring in evidence that Grim had received past complaints that the parking lot surface was slippery. Grim wanted the statements excluded as hearsay.

Issue: Are the complaints admissible?
Holding: page 113

80. Acting Guilty

Facts: Morgan was accused of murdering Wigmore. Morgan's defense was that Webster had actually killed

Wigmore. After the murder, but before the trial, Webster killed himself. Morgan wanted to have the suicide admitted as evidence of Webster's admission of guilt.

Issue: Is the suicide admissible for that purpose?
Holding: page 113

81. Attorney-Client Privilege

Facts: Woody failed to show up for his trial. The United States government wanted to charge Woody for bail jumping and tried to have the court compel Woody's lawyer to testify as to whether he told Woody about the trial date.

Issue: Is the information privileged?
Holding: page 114

82. Assertions of Fact

Facts: Andrew was suspected of conducting illegal betting operations. The police had a search warrant for his home, and while they were conducting a search, an officer answered the telephone (an act covered by the warrant). The caller gave instructions for placing certain bets at sporting events.

Bet on Sea Biscuit in the Fourth

Search Warrant

Issue: Are the statements admissible?
Holding: page 114

83. For Better or Worse

Facts: Hy and his wife Mary Jane were arrested for drug smuggling. Mary Jane was not indicted because she agreed to testify against Hy regarding certain activities that she had witnessed. Hy's attorney objected to Mary Jane's testimony being used because of the "spousal privilege."

Issue: Is Mary Jane's testimony admissible?
Holding: page 114

84. Best Evidence

Facts: Sarah was suing Charlie for injuries. Dr. Rado X-rayed Sarah and then sent the X-rays to Sarah's treating physician. At trial, Dr. Rado took the stand to testify about the X-rays. He no longer had them in his possession, so he referred to his written report to refresh his recollection about the results. Sarah's attorney did not explain to the court why the original X-rays were not presented in court.

Issue: Is the report admissible?
Holding: page 115

85. Refreshed Recollection

Facts: Roxanne and her husband had a heated argument, which ended with him being shot by Roxanne. At Roxanne's murder trial, expert testimony was given that the gun was faulty and could fire without pulling the trigger. Roxanne had only a fuzzy memory of the event, but under hypnosis performed by a reliable expert recalled that her finger was not on the trigger when it went off. The court excluded Roxanne's recollections because a state law prohibited any "hypnotically refreshed" testimony.

Issue: Should the testimony have been admitted?
Holding: page 115

CRIMINAL PROCEDURE

86. Home Sweet Home

Facts: Chip committed a burglary, and the police found him at home and arrested him there. They didn't have a search warrant, but they searched the house and found evidence to support the belief that Chip had committed the burglary.

Issue: Was the search legal?
Holding: page 115

87. Fruit of the Poisonous Tree

Facts: Hugh and Louis went to Drew's rented apartment to do a drug deal. They were there for a few hours weighing and bagging up cocaine. Based on a reliable tip from an informant, the police went to Drew's house and saw these activities through a window. The cocaine was later seized, and Hugh, Louis, and Drew were arrested.

Issue: A: Can the seized cocaine be used against Hugh and Louis? B: Against Drew?
Holding: page 116

88. Going Solo

Facts: Freddy was arrested for stealing cars. He petitioned the court to represent himself. The court approved, but after the trial began, decided that Freddy was not qualified to be his own lawyer. An attorney was appointed and Freddy was convicted.

Issue: Should Freddy have a new trial?
Holding: page 116

89. Defective Counsel

Facts: The charge was mail fraud. The court-appointed attorney was a young real estate lawyer who was given 25 days to prepare for trial. The defendant was convicted. There is no evidence that the attorney made any errors at the trial.

Issue: Was the defendant denied the right to effective assistance of counsel?
Holding: page 116

90. Lineup

Facts: Wayne was formally charged with bank robbery. The evidence against him was primarily witness identification. The lineup in which Wayne was identified took place after he had been charged. Wayne's attorney wasn't present during the lineup, nor had Wayne been asked if he wanted his attorney there.

Issue: Did Wayne have a right to counsel at the lineup?
Holding: page 117

91. Plain View

Facts: Officer Bobby obtained a proper warrant to search Horace's home for the proceeds of a robbery that Horace had allegedly committed. While searching, Officer Bobby didn't find the proceeds, but during his search saw in plain view the weapons that were used in the crime and took them as evidence.

Issue: Are the weapons admissible at trial?
Holding: page 117

EMPLOYMENT AND LABOR

92. Reverse Discrimination

Facts: Mickey, Ricky, and Dickey worked for a trucking company. They improperly took some of the goods that were supposed to have been shipped to customers and, as a result, the company fired Mickey and Ricky, who were white. Dickey, who was black, wasn't fired.

Issue: Did the company violate antidiscrimination laws?
Holding: page 117

93. Discriminating Effect

Facts: Massachusetts enacted a law to help military veterans get government jobs. The law gave veterans priority over nonveterans for consideration for hiring. Since most military veterans were men, the law practically excluded women from getting jobs with the state.

Issue: Is the law illegal?
Holding: page 117

94. Fertile Grounds

Facts: Dumco, a battery manufacturer, had a company policy that women who could bear children (regardless of whether they were pregnant or planned to have children) could not work in positions where they would be exposed to lead, which is dangerous to an unborn fetus. Female employees had to provide proof to the company that they were incapable of having children in order to apply for one of those positions.

Issue: Does Dumco have a good defense for this discriminatory practice?
Holding: page 118

95. Affirmative Action

Facts: Connecticut required a written exam for employees to be promoted to supervisor in the welfare department. Statistics showed that a very small proportion of black employees passed the exam compared with other racial or ethnic groups. John, Paul, George, and Richard, who were black, took the test and failed and were not promoted. They sued the state. The state argued that it had other selection processes that were more favorable to black employees and resulted in other blacks being promoted, so its overall policies were fair.

Issue: Is the state's policy discriminatory?
Holding: page 118

96. Uninvited Pest

Facts: At work, Marilyn's boss, Ollie, constantly talked about sex, made lewd remarks and gestures, and asked Marilyn to watch dirty movies with him. He also tried to get her to go on a date with him and, when she refused, he made comments to her that seemed to threaten her job security. One day, some nude photos of Marilyn appeared in a motorcycle magazine and people at work saw them. Ollie told Marilyn that the other employees no longer wanted Marilyn at the company, and that if she didn't go out with him, he might have her fired. Marilyn sued for sexual harassment, claiming that Ollie's behavior was "uninvited and offensive."

Issue: Do the nude photos help Ollie's case?
Holding: page 119

97. Legal Discrimination

Facts: Frank was from the Philippines. He applied for a clerk's job at the Department of Motor Vehicles in the state of Hawaii. He had the highest score on the written test for the job. When he was interviewed, the interviewer noted that because of Frank's accent, he would have difficulty communicating with the public, which would be a big part of his job. The job went to another applicant, who had scored lower on the test.

Issue: Was Frank illegally discriminated against?
Holding: page 119

98. Qualified Individuals

Facts: Maggie had a serious hearing problem—she could understand speech only through lip-reading. Maggie applied to a college for entry in its nursing program. She was otherwise qualified, but the college denied admission to Maggie because she had to be able to understand important medical instructions from doctors as part of the clinical portion of the program.

Issue: Did the college illegally discriminate against Maggie?
Holding: page 119

99. Labor Dispute

Facts: The television technical workers union was in negotiation with a television station. When both sides could not reach agreement, union workers picketed the station while off duty. The negotiations continued to stall, so the workers printed up flyers stating that the television station gave "second-rate" service, and distributed the flyers to the public. The television station fired the workers while the labor dispute was still active.

Issue: Does the station have to reinstate the workers?
Holding: page 119

100. Accommodations

Facts: Vanessa was confined to a wheelchair. She worked for a state agency that had lowered a sink in a bathroom near her workspace and bought adjustable furniture for her, but there was a sink in the employee coffee room that remained too high for Vanessa to use. Also, because of her illness, Vanessa experienced occasional complications that made it impossible for her to go to the office for extended periods. The agency tried to accommodate a flexible schedule and reduced workload. However, it rejected Vanessa's request to lower the coffee room sink, buy her a computer for home use, and allow her to work full-time from home during her bouts.

Issue: Does the agency have to accommodate Vanessa's requests?
Holding: page 120

101. Union Rules

Facts: Lonnie was an official elected by the union members. When the union proposed increasing union dues, Lonnie spoke out openly against the increase. The union leaders fired him for this.

Issue: Did the union improperly fire Lonnie?
Holding: page 120

FAMILY LAW

102. Marriage License

Facts: Romeo and Juliet were married in a religious ceremony. They had no marriage license from the state where they lived. The state required both, but did not expressly make a marriage without a state license void. Juliet sought to have the marriage dissolved, but the court said it was invalid, so they had no legal jurisdiction to dissolve the marriage.

Issue: Is the marriage valid?
Holding: page 121

103. Husbands' Rights

Facts: Paul and Jane were separated but not divorced. They lived in separate apartments, and they each owned their own apartment. One time Paul broke through Jane's door, entered the apartment without her permission, and slapped her around.

Issue: Can Paul be guilty of burglary in his wife's home?
Holding: page 121

104. Split the Baby

Facts: Alan was married to Janet for about 40 years. For 24 of those years until he died, he was also married to Debbie. Debbie had believed in good faith that Alan was divorced when she married him. During these years, Alan had two families, participated in both of them, had good relations with both wives, and made a lot of money in business. When he died without a will, Debbie sought a share of his assets.

Issues: A: Is Debbie and Alan's marriage void? B: Is Debbie entitled to inherit anything?
Holding: page 121

105. Marital Property

Facts: During their marriage, Orson gave Una expensive jewels for birthdays and holidays. During their divorce proceedings, a court had to determine which property was to be considered "marital property" that would be divided between Orson and Una. They excluded the jewelry, deciding that since these were gifts, they belonged only to Una. During the proceedings, Orson explained that, even though the jewels had been given at special times, he had actually purchased them as investments.

Issue: Does Una keep the jewelry?
Holding: page 121

106. Parents' Rights

Facts: Jonas and Wally were members of an old and well-established religion. They believed that sending their children to school beyond the eighth grade would interfere with their ability to educate them in a manner consistent with their religious beliefs, and might even endanger their children's spiritual salvation. So Jonas and Wally removed their children from school and continued to educate them in a way that would help the children become productive members of their religious society. They were fined for violating their state's compulsory education law.

Issue: A: Can Jonas and Wally direct their children's lives this way?
B: Is the state law constitutional?
Holding: page 122

107. Family Ties

Facts: Johnny and Lori, who were not married, had a baby, Jessie. The couple's relationship ended, and Lori married Rich soon after. When Jessie was two, Rich sought to adopt her. Up to that point, Johnny had no contact with Jessie and had not provided any financial support or acted as a father to Jessie. He also had not registered himself as Jessie's father on the state registry, which exists so that fathers in these types of circumstances can be notified of adoption proceedings and have an opportunity to be heard. Nor was Johnny's name on Jessie's birth certificate, which would have triggered his right to receive notice. Therefore, Rich's adoption of Jessie was finalized without Johnny having a say in the matter.

Issue: Does Johnny have the right to be heard at the adoption hearing?
Holding: page 123

HOLDINGS

1. Best Laid Plans
Yes. They had taken "substantial steps" toward commission of the crime, showing a "criminal purpose." They had passed beyond the stage of mere preparation.
United States v. Jackson, 560 F.2d 112 (1977)

2. Vain Attempt
No. David only took steps of preparation. Solicitation of another to commit a crime does not always rise to an attempt without additional steps. Courts have varied views about what steps must be taken for a solicitation to be considered an "attempt."
State v. Davis, 6 S.W.2d 609 (1928)

3. Take the Money and Run
No. To be guilty of larceny, one must take property with intent to permanently deprive the owner of it. Cheeky did not deprive Big Bucks of the collected money. Also, taking the "economic benefit" was not larceny because Cheeky lawfully had the money for 72 hours under contract, so the bank would not have had a right to the economic benefit during that time. Cheeky might be liable to Big Bucks for fraud.
People v. Jennings, 504 N.E.2d 1079 (1986)

4. Ex Post Facto

No. Albert acted on the latest court ruling, which said his acts were protected. The United States Constitution prohibits "ex post facto laws"—laws that make an earlier action, which was innocent when it was committed, criminal.

United States v. Albertini, 830 F.2d 985 (1987)

5. Drunk Again

A: No. B: No.

While an alcoholic may be unable to control the compulsion to drink, and it cannot be a crime to be an alcoholic, the court found that there was no evidence that a chronic alcoholic has the compulsion to drink in public. It would be illogical to excuse behavior that in some complex sense may have been the result of the irresistible compulsion to drink. The defendant in this case was relying on a prior case that held that it was "cruel and unusual" to convict a person solely for the status of being a drug addict. The court distinguished the cases in that here Bill was not being convicted merely for his status.

Powell v. Texas, 392 U.S. 514 (1968)

6. Russian Roulette

Yes. Malcolm did not intend to kill Billy, but he intentionally shot him. He should have known that his reckless act could kill Billy, making it equivalent to intending to kill. Some states have laws including reckless murder under the definition of intentional murder.

Commonwealth v. Malone, 47 A.2d 445 (1946)

7. Possession Is Nine-Tenths of the Law

No. A seller who refuses or fails to deliver goods sold to his or her purchaser is not guilty of larceny. The property was removed by Bill and Linda while they still owned it. However, they may be guilty of fraud.

Commonwealth v. Tluchak, 70 A.2d 657 (1950)

8. Self-Defense

No. Benny cannot claim self-defense since he provoked the incident and never communicated the intent to back down.

United States v. Peterson, 483 F.2d 1222 (1973)

9. Vicarious Kill

Yes. Bob's murder was the result of the shop owner's act of self-defense. Although the shop owner's wife fired first, Bob and Bert provoked the shooting. Therefore, Larry, being an accomplice and a co-conspirator to the robbery, was guilty of the murder of Bob through "vicarious liability," even though he sat in the car.

Taylor v. Superior Court of Alameda County, 477 P.2d 131 (1970)

10. Drunk and Disorderly

No. To be guilty of a crime, one has to voluntarily commit the crime. Mickey did not voluntarily go into public. The police arrested him and then took him to the highway.

Martin v. State, 17 So. 2d. 427 (1944)

11. Scared to Death

Yes. This is classic felony murder, where a homicide is the direct causal result of a separate felony, even though murder was not initially intended. The underlying principle of the felony murder rule is that when committing inherently dangerous crimes, it is a foreseeable risk that a death may result even if death is not intended. That the victim was ill and may have died soon from his condition does not absolve Terry from causing his death prematurely.

People v. Stamp, 2 Cal. App. 3d 203 (1969)

12. The Drunkard's Defense

Yes. Voluntary intoxication is not by itself a defense, but it may be a defense to a crime that requires a specific intent, such as intentional murder. Even if Alan did not have the intent to murder, he could have been found guilty of assault, or reckless murder (had the officer died).

Roberts v. People, 19 Mich. 401 (1870)

13. Cruise Control

No. Joe is responsible for speeding because his speeding was not purely involuntary. Unlike an unexpected malfunction such as failure of an essential component of a vehicle (e.g. brake failure), cruise control is a device to which the driver delegates partial control of the vehicle.

State v. Baker, 571 P.2d 65 (1977)

14. Depraved Heart

A: Yes. B: No

Although Ian was drunk and he did not intend to kill anyone, he operated his car in a manner that disregarded the lives and safety of others, and therefore can be convicted of murder. The court found that this behavior was distinguished from the majority of drunk-driving cases where the drunk driver is reckless because he or she is driving with impaired abilities, rather than wantonly and intentionally putting the lives of others at risk. This is consistent with the holdings of most United States courts—that such a level of recklessness can support a murder conviction.

United States v. Fleming, 739 F.2d 945 (1984)

15. Duty to Save

No. People do not have a legal duty to save each other's lives unless there is a special legal relationship, such as for parent and child, contracting parties, a statutorily imposed duty, or the duty of a landowner to guests.

People v. Beardsley, 113 N.W. 1128 (1907)

16. Just Hanging Around

No. Mere presence at the scene of a crime without assisting in some way does not establish criminal liability. Fleeing is not enough, either. The person must actually help, for example, by being a lookout.

State v. Vaillancourt, 453 A.2d 1327 (1982)

17. Time of Death

No. Since the evidence did not show beyond a reasonable doubt that Rose's leaving the scene caused Milt's death, Rose could not be convicted of manslaughter. However, Rose is guilty of leaving the scene of an accident.

State v. Rose, 311 A.2d. 281 (1973)

18. Audacious Auditor

No. To be guilty of fraud, one must make improper use of the property to cause damage to, in this case, either the IRS or a particular individual whose information was obtained. Zeb violated agency policy, but going no further, he can't be guilty of fraud.

United States v. Czubinski, 106 F.3d 1069
(1st Cir. 1997)

19. Sharp Shopper

Yes. Even though Matthew did not permanently deprive the store of the shirt, taking the shirt to another department with intent to get a refund was tantamount to intending to deprive the shop of the *value* of the shirt, if not the actual shirt. The court found that if the refund attempt had failed, there was a substantial risk that Matthew would have ultimately permanently deprived the store of the shirt itself, by leaving the store with it, to avoid a "scene" in the store.

People v. Davis, 965 P.2d 1165 (1998)

20. Legal Fees?

Yes. Graham fraudulently induced (i.e., tricked) Frank to give him the money to be used for a special purpose (to bribe the police), intending to keep the money for himself. Even though Frank gave up possession of the money, title remained with Frank until the purpose for which it was supposed to be used was accomplished.

Graham v. United States, 187 F.2d 87 (1950)

21. Wildfire

Yes. Although Artie did not start the fire on the second floor, the death was reasonably related to the arson on the fifth floor and could have been foreseen.

People v. Arzon, 401 N.Y.S.2d 156 (1978)

22. Money Bags

Yes. Jim took the money intending to permanently deprive the banks of ownership. It was irrelevant that Jim had custody of the money when he took it.

United States v. Mafnas, 701 F.2d 83 (9th Cir. 1983)

23. False Pretenses

Yes. By using the ATM machine knowing the card was invalid, Andy made an implied false representation. That the transaction was separately approved does not negate the shop's reliance on Andy's misrepresentation.

People v. Whight, 43 Cal. Rptr. 2d 163 (1995)

24. This Land Is My Land

No. An offer is open until it is revoked or accepted. Joel, by his actions, revoked the offer when he offered and sold the land to Sylvia before Adele accepted his offer (and the revocation is valid even if it wasn't communicated to Adele until after she believed she had accepted the offer).

Dickinson v. Dodds, 2 Ch. D 463 (1876)

25. Just Reward

No. For a contract, there must be an offer and acceptance. An offeree must know of the offer in order to accept. Mary could not be said to have accepted the reward offer, because she was not aware of it when she informed the police of Clyde's whereabouts.

Glover v. Jewish War Veterans of United States, 68 A.2d 233 (1949)

26. Family Values

Yes. For a valid contract, each party must give something to the other in exchange for what they receive, called "consideration." This can be money, performance of an act, or a promise to do, or not do, something.

Hamer v. Sidway, 27 N.E. 256 (1891)

27. Minor Infraction

Yes. A minor may void a contract during the time the minor is still under the age of 18. The exception is where a minor enters into a contract for "necessaries" such as shelter, food, or medical attention.

Bowling v. Sperry, 184 N.E.2d 901 (1962)

28. What's Wrong With This Picture?

Yes. Even though a minor can disaffirm a contract made by the minor, the minor can't disaffirm the contract made by the parent on behalf of the minor, where the parent was considered to have been protecting the minor's interest at the time. Note that in this case, an injunction was obtained so that the photos could not be used in pornographic publications.

Brooke Shields v. Gross, 461 N.Y.2d 254 (1983)

29. Dominion and Control

No. To make a valid gift (or "assignment"), one must intend to give a gift and must deliver an item (which can be symbolic) that completely strips the owner of "dominion or control." Rebecca intended to give a gift, but the paper she gave was not clear evidence of ownership (it was too informal). Nor did Rebecca write anything on the paper evidencing her intent to give over the money. Rebecca still had control and could have retrieved the money from Tony (had she still been alive), so the heirs get the money.

Cook v. Lum, 26 A. 803 (1893)

30. Promises, Promises

No. There was no contract here because there was no "consideration." Marion made the promise in exchange for a past act.

Mills v. Wyman, 20 Mass. (3 Pick.) 207 (1825)

31. Do IOU?

No. Taylor made a promise to Henry based on an act already done. Even though morally Taylor should continue to pay Henry, there is no contract right because there was no "consideration" (or promise) from Henry to do or provide anything in exchange for the payments.

Harrington v. Taylor, 36 S.E.2d 227 (1945)

32. You Dance Divinely

Yes. Generally one must make a misrepresentation of "fact" for it to be actionable. But an "opinion" is actionable if the other party does not have an equal opportunity to learn the truth and the disclosing

party has "superior knowledge." Note that Gene did not have a duty to tell Ginger that her dancing ability was poor—he could have said nothing. But once he decided to give an opinion, he was required to tell "the whole truth."
Vokes v. Arthur Murray, Inc., 212 So. 2d 906 (1968)

33. Oops!

Yes. A good-faith mistake is not a defense to an intentional act that causes harm or loss to another.
Ranson v. Kitner, 31 Ill. App. 241 (1889)

34. Trespasser Traps

No. A person may protect property from trespassers using reasonable force. Force that can kill or seriously injure may not be used to protect property. It may be used only in self-defense or in defense of others.
Katko v. Briney, 183 N.W. 2d 657 (1971)

35. What a Buzz

No. The broken buzzer was not the "proximate" cause of Robin's injury. A violent crime is not, in general, the reasonably foreseeable outcome of a broken buzzer.
Medcalf v. Washington Heights Condominium Association, Inc., 747 A.2d 532 (2000)

36. Just Blowing Smoke

Yes. A "battery" is an intentional, offensive touching of another person. Blowing smoke in someone's face

can be considered "offensive," and the particles in smoke are sufficiently able to "touch" a person. The court considered deliberately blowing smoke different than breathing ordinary secondhand smoke.
Leichtman v. WLW Jacor Communications, Inc., Inc., 634 N.E.2d 697 (1994)

37. Pole Fault
Yes. The maker or distributor of a product must consider where the product will be used when designing or distributing it. Here Eddie's Electric Company should have made sure it did not use a pole that couldn't resist impact from a car, since the pole was being placed in a heavily trafficked area.
Bernier v. Boston Edison Co., 403 N.E.2d 391 (1980)

38. Emotional Distress
No. In order to be entitled to damages for emotional distress, Barbara would have had to be in the "zone of danger," observe the accident when it happened, and suffer distress that would have been different from that suffered by a disinterested bystander (i.e., not a family member).
Thing v. La Chusa, 771 P.2d 814 (1989)

39. Proximate Cause
A: No. B: Yes.
The bus driver's breach of his duty to follow the traffic law did not cause the accident. The brake failure

on the truck caused the accident. This is an "independent supervening cause," which breaks the chain of "proximate" cause (the foreseeable chain of events) required for negligence. On the other hand, the owner of the truck was negligent, because the brake failure was the proximate cause of the accident.
Sheehan v. City of New York, New York, 354 N.E.2d 832 (1976)

40. Do I Do?
Yes. Medical doctors, including psychiatrists, have a duty to warn potential victims about the violent intentions of their patients, regardless of doctor-patient privilege.
Tarasoff v. Regents of the University of California, 13 Cal. 3d 177 (1974)

41. Please Release Me
No. A release of one wrongdoer by a plaintiff, if given in good faith, discharges the wrongdoer from liability to the plaintiff and also to another wrongdoer.
Slocum v. Donahue, 693 N.E.2d 179 (1998)

42. Public or Private?
No. Receiving information that one knows has been improperly gained does not constitute an invasion of privacy. Also, facts about a political career are not "private facts," which are the subject of invasion of privacy suits.

Pearson v. Dodd, 410 F.2d 701 (D.C. Cir. 1969); cert. denied, 395 U.S. 947 (1969)

43. Private Parts
No. A private individual's right to privacy is not absolute. Publication that is newsworthy is protected and does not violate the right to privacy.
Cape Publications, Inc. v. Bridges, 423 So.2d 426 (1982)

44. A Shot in the Dark
Yes. It is certain that either Gene or Mark caused the damage, and it would be unfair for Tom not to recover damages simply because he could not prove which one. It is up to Gene or Mark to prove he didn't do it, and, if they both can't, then they are mutually liable.
Summers v. Tice, 33 Cal. 2d 80 (1948)

45. Spam
Yes. This is a trespass on personal property—a substantial interference or intermeddling with another's possession.
Compuserve Inc. v. Cyber Promotions, Inc., 962 F. Supp. 1015 (1997)

46. Flight from Reality

Yes. One who experiences a sudden onset of insanity (like an unpredictable physical attack) has no way of guarding against possible negligent acts. However, the general rule is that those suffering from *preexisting* or *permanent* insanity will not be relieved of liability for negligence because: 1) someone has to bear responsibility, and it shouldn't be a completely innocent party; 2) those interested in an insane person's estate should take care to control and restrain the insane; and 3) doing so would otherwise encourage false claims of insanity.

Breunig v. American Family Insurance Company, 173 N.W.2d 619 (1970)

47. What a Drag

Yes. Jeff was "acting in concert" with Norm in the drag race, so even though his car never hit Larry's, he was liable for causing the damage. To be a joint "tortfeasor," you only have to encourage or aid the activity, not actually cause the harm.

Bierczynski v. Rogers, 239 A.2d 218 (1968)

48. To Be or Not to Be

Yes. A negligent person can be liable for another's suicide if the suicide was the result of a mental disturbance that results substantially from the negligent act and destroys the will to live. The court found that even though Dr. Bob intended to kill himself, he still was suffering from an irresistible impulse that

was substantially caused by the accident.
Fuller v. Preis, 332 N.E.2d 263, 363 N.Y.S. 3d 568 (1974)

49. Hands Off
No. Rupert was an independent contractor. If he had been an employee of Okay Publishing, then Okay would likely have had liability. The difference is that employers have more direction and control over the actions and manner and method of work of employees than of independent contractors.
Murrell v. Goertz, 597 P.2d 1223 (1979)

50. Party Animals
No. While an adult who serves a minor alcohol can be held liable for injuries resulting from that minor's drunkenness, a minor cannot be held liable for injuries that result from serving alcohol to another minor. Minors, whether they serve or consume, are considered incompetent under the law to handle alcohol. Note that this is a state supreme court case, and a federal district court later held differently, but the state court disagreed.
Kapres v. Heller, 640 A.2d 888 (1994)

51. Last Call
Yes. A restaurant can be held liable for damages to third parties for negligently serving alcohol. Note that this is a matter of state law, and many state

courts have taken this position, but the rules and factors vary from state to state.

Brigance v. Velvet Dove Restaurant, 725 P.2d 300 (1986)

52. Blood on the Tracks

No. A property owner has no duty of care to a trespasser until he is aware of his presence. Manuel was trespassing—he was not at a public crossing. Fast Track Railroad Company had no knowledge that Manuel was there until it was too late to exercise any care.

Sheehan v. St. Paul & Duluth Ry. Co., 76 F. 201
(7th Cir. 1896)

53. Public Figure

No. The trial court found the *Times* liable, but the Supreme Court reversed the decision. Because Sully was a public official, the *Times* did not have to prove the ad was true in all respects, but that it was published "without malice" or "reckless disregard for the truth." The ad was substantially true, and any inaccuracies were trivial. This standard for libel against public officials is different than for private individuals, because the First Amendment of the United States Constitution is based on the need for a free flow of ideas in society, especially debate about government activity. Also, public officials should expect comment and criticism as part of their jobs.

New York Times Co. v. Sullivan, 376 U.S. 254 (1964)

54. Fair Trial

Yes. For a court to close a trial to protect a defendant's Sixth Amendment right to a fair trial, there must be compelling findings by the court that having a public trial would prejudice the defendant. Here, there were no such findings.

Richmond Newspapers v. Virginia, 448 U.S. 555 (1980)

55. What Is a Taking?

No. The Fifth Amendment requires that the government pay "just compensation" for a taking of private property. However, a state exercising its police power may "regulate" the use of property, which does not constitute a "taking" under the Fifth Amendment.

Miller v. Schoene, 276 U.S. 272 (1928)

56. I Know It When I See It

Yes. The legislature may prohibit dissemination of obscenity to consenting adults because such expressions of "speech" are not protected by the First Amendment. Courts have struggled to define what constitutes obscenity.

Paris Adult Theatre I v. Slaton, 413 U.S. 49 (1973)

57. Immediate Lawless Action

Yes. For speech advocating violence to be punishable, it must be directed at inciting immediate lawless action and likely to produce such action. Teaching or advocating violence is not the same as pushing a group to violent action. The statute under which Mr. Lily was originally prosecuted punished advocacy alone. Therefore, the statute was found to be unconstitutional.

Brandenburg v. Ohio, 395 U.S. 444 (1969)

58. Alien Rights

No. Although a public education is not a fundamental right protected by the United States Constitution, it is an important right. For a state to deny an important right, the reason must be "rationally related to a substantial state interest." The court did not think that Texas' reasons were substantial state interests. It was also judged unfair to deny children an education due to their immigration status, since they did not voluntarily come to the United States illegally.

Plyer v. Doe, 457 U.S. 202 (1982)

59. Double Standard

No. This rule violates "equal protection." Those similarly situated should be treated the same by the law. The rule was based on an outmoded notion that widows were considered dependent but widowers were not.

Califano v. Goldfarb, 430 U.S. 199 (1977)

60. Losers Weepers

No. This is not a case of "finders keepers, losers weepers," because the property was "mislaid," not lost. Rather, possession of mislaid property lies with the owner of the premises where it is found. These common-law rules are well established. Most states have statutes addressing the rules regarding rights to found property.

Benjamin v. Lindner Aviation, Inc., 534 N.W. 2d 400 (1995)

61. Stair Master

No. Gretta owns the encroached property through "adverse possession," even though when she built the stairs she did not know that her possession was "hostile." Traditionally one had to know of the encroachment for adverse possession to occur. But many courts and legislatures have abandoned this requirement since it places an intentional wrongdoer in a better position than an innocent one. The other requirements for adverse possession are that it must be open, continuous, and exclusive. Here, Gretta's use of the stairs met the other requirements.

Manillo v. Gorski, 255 A.2d 258 (1969)

62. The Issue of Tissue

No. A person does not have a property right in his or her "tissue." Dr. Noall *was* liable to Roger for breach of fiduciary duty for not telling Roger about the research. There are also public policy issues that the court cited—e.g., if tissue ownership were a legal right, it could interfere with important research being conducted for the benefit of society.

Moore v. Regents of the University of California, 793 P.2d 479 (1990)

63. Self-Help

Yes. The right of re-entry does not permit a landlord to enter a tenant's home without consent and to take the tenant's belongings. A landlord may seek judicial help to enforce the right to repossess the premises. The forcible entry in this case was considered "self-help," which was not justified because the landlord had a proper legal remedy. (The dissenting judges thought entering with a key was not "forcible.")

Jordon v. Talbot, 361 P.2d 20 (1961)

64. Quiet Enjoyment

A: Yes. B: No.

When a landlord causes or fails to remedy a situation that interferes with "quiet enjoyment," tenants may vacate without liability for rent. This is called "constructive eviction."

Blacket v. Olanoff, 358 N.E.2d 817 (1977)

65. Running with the Land

Yes. When one purchases land, he or she is deemed to accept any restrictions that are publicly recorded before the sale. Such restrictions "run with the land." Also, homeowners who rely on recorded restrictions when they purchase a property need assurance that their neighbors will be complying with the same rules.

Citizens for Covenant Compliance v. Anderson, 906 P.2d 1314 (1995)

66. Right of Publicity

Yes. Though Brown's "likeness" did not appear in the ad (the requirement under California law), the Court found that the robot portrayed Brown's "identity" under the common law "right of publicity." Sam's argued that it had a First Amendment right to parody Brown, but the court rejected this defense since the ad was used for commercial purposes, not entertainment.

White v. Samsung, 971 F.2d 1395 (1992)

67. Pig Tale

Yes. The two requirements to show copyright infringement are access to the work and using such access to copy the work. Access and copying can be inferred the more that a work resembles an already copyrighted work and is unlike anything in the public domain, because it is less likely to have been an independent creation.

Ty, Inc. v. GMA Accessories, Inc., 132 F.3d 1167 (7th Cir. 1997)

68. Great Idea!

Yes. Even though ideas are not copyrightable, a party can agree to pay for an idea. If the court found that Bolder did not accept the contract, and Bolder did independent research of the event without using Brian's synopsis, Brian would not be entitled to payment.

Desny v. Wilder, 46 Cal. 2d 715 (1956)

69. Program Protection

Yes. A computer program is protectable by copyright because it is an expression of an idea fixed in tangible form. Dr. Buck had obviously had access to the program in order to copy it. Dr. Buck did not argue that he didn't copy the program—he argued that the program was not entitled to protection.

Whelan Associates, Inc. v. Jaslow Dental Lab, Inc., 797 F.2d 1222 (3d. Cir. 1986)

70. Trade Secret

Yes. DoWell's process was a trade secret, which it took appropriate steps to protect. The flight alone was not improper, and Chris did not physically "trespass" on DoWell's property, but Chris obtained knowledge of DoWell's secret through "improper means."

E.J. DuPont Denemours & Co. v. Rolfe Christopher et al., 431 F.2d 1012 (5th Cir. 1970); cert. denied, 400 U.S. 1024 (1971)

71. Public Display

Yes. This is an unauthorized public display of a copyrighted work. The right to publicly perform a work is part of the "bundle of rights" that comes with copyright. While Fairview did not actually perform the work, it allowed its customers to do so and therefore authorized the public performance in violation of the copyright.

Columbia Pictures Industries, Inc. v. Aveco, Inc., 800 F.2d 59 (3d Cir. 1986)

72. That's My Color!

Yes. A color can become distinctive enough to associate it with a particular product or manufacturer, and can therefore be registered as a trademark.
Qualitex Co. v. Jacobson Products Co., Inc.,
34 U.S.P.Q.2d. 1161 (1995)

73. Hanky-Panky

Yes. Hank was suffering from an "insane delusion." There was no reasonable basis for him to believe that his wife was unfaithful. Therefore, he was not "competent" to make the will. If Hank had merely been "mistaken," that is, if there had been some facts on which he could base his conclusion, even if it was wrong, the will would have been valid.
In re Honigman, 203 N.Y.S.2d 859 (1960)

74. Virtual Parents

Yes. The doctrine is "Equitable Adoption." Even with no written adoption agreement, an "agreement" can be inferred by circumstances. Peter and Virginia raised Megan as their own child and told her she was adopted.
Matter of Heirs of Hodge, 470 So. 2d 740 (1985)

75. Brotherly Love

No. Jacob Sr. had disposed of the land during his life, intending that it satisfied the bequest in the will. This is "ademption"—meaning that the property is no longer part of the estate.

In re Estate of Wolff, 349 N.W.2d 33 (1984)

76. Hear Ye, Hear Ye

Yes. The will was signed in the testator's presence since they were in constant contact. Otherwise, the testator's wishes would have been invalidated on a highly technical point. Courts seek to make sure that a testator's wishes prevail.

Cunningham v. Cunningham, 83 N.W. 58 (1900)

77. The Paper Chase

A: Yes. B: Yes.

The memorandum was properly "incorporated by reference" into the will. The notebook, although it was not in existence at the time the will was made, was in existence at the time the codicils (amendments) were added, so the notebook was considered to be "in existence" at the time of the original will and, therefore, incorporated by reference.

Clark v. Greenhalge, 582 N.E.2d 949 (1991)

78. What's in a Name?

A: No. B: No.

The bequest is not invalid, because on its face it appears clear. There is a "latent ambiguity" because there is no "wife" named Mabel Smith, and the person who was once known as Mabel Smith is not the wife. The court found that Johanna loved Evelyn and had had no contact with Mabel for years. She had merely mistakenly put the name "Mabel" in her will and had meant to leave half the estate to Evelyn.

Breckheimer v. Kraft, Kraft, 273 N.E.2d 468 (1971)

79. What Is Hearsay, Anyway?

Yes. Third-party statements are not considered hearsay if they are being offered only to show that the statements were made, not whether the statements themselves are true assertions of fact. Here the statement was admissible to show that Grim had knowledge of prior complaints.

Vinyard v. Vinyard Funeral Home, Inc., 435 S.W.2d 392 (1968)

80. Acting Guilty

Yes. Conduct can be used as evidence of a "statement" to communicate an idea. The conduct must be reviewed to see if it is probative of the issue in question. Here, the court found that guilt could be inferred from Webster's suicide. The court did not address the issue of whether the statement should be excluded as hearsay.

Commonwealth v. Knapp, VII Amer. St. Trials 395 (1830)

81. Attorney-Client Privilege

No. The attorney-client privilege does not apply to a communication about date and time of trial. The privilege applies to communications between the client and the attorney for the purpose of seeking and receiving legal advice. Also, this communication was information given, not by the client, but by the court, to the attorney.

United States v. Woodruff, 383 F. Supp. 696 (1974)

82. Assertions of Fact

Yes. These statements are not hearsay because they were not made for the purpose of asserting that Andrew was engaging in illegal betting activity. However, it could be inferred from the caller giving betting instructions that Andrew was a bookmaker, so they are admissible.

United States v. Zenni, 492 F. Supp. 464 (1980)

83. For Better or Worse

Yes. The privilege to not give adverse testimony against a spouse belongs to the testifying spouse, not to the spouse who is charged. Mary Jane cannot be compelled to testify against Hy, but she can voluntarily do so. The spousal privilege once provided that a spouse could not give adverse testimony without the consent of both spouses. However, most states and evidence rules have abolished this rule and follow this case. Note, however, that confidential communications between spouses (which are different than providing adverse testimony) cannot be divulged in court without the consent of both parties.

Trammel v. United States, 445 U.S. 40 (1980)

84. Best Evidence

No. The "best evidence" rule requires an original writing to be produced if one is seeking to admit documentary evidence, unless a satisfactory reason is provided for its absence. Here, the X-ray was the original, it was not produced, and no satisfactory reason for its absence was given to the court.

Sirico v. Cotto, 67 Misc. 2d 636 (1971)

85. Refreshed Recollection

Yes. It is unconstitutional for a state law to prohibit a defendant's testimony if it is otherwise reliable and corroborated. Defendants have a constitutional right to testify on their own behalf.

Rock v. Arkansas, 483 U.S. 44 (1987)

86. Home Sweet Home

No. Police may make a search incident to a lawful arrest, but it is limited to the suspect's person and the immediate area where a suspect could reach for a weapon or evidence.

Chimel v. California, 395 U.S. 752 (1969)

87. Fruit of the Poisonous Tree

A: Yes. B: No.

Drew had a reasonable expectation of privacy in his apartment because it was his home. Therefore, the police's "search" through the window was unreasonable. However, Hugh and Louis did not have an expectation of privacy because it was not their home, nor were they legitimate overnight or social guests. They were there briefly to conduct illegal acts. So, the officers' "search" was not unreasonable with respect to Hugh and Louis, and the cocaine subsequently obtained was not considered "fruit of the poisonous tree."

Minnesota v. Carter, 525 U.S. 83 (1998)

88. Going Solo

Yes. An accused in a criminal proceeding has a constitutional right to self-representation. This derives from the Fifth Amendment right of a defendant to confront witnesses. A court cannot deny this right even if it feels the defendant is not a "good lawyer."

Faretta v. California, 422 U.S. 806 (1975)

89. Defective Counsel

No. There can be no presumption of ineffective counsel based on age, experience, or preparation time. The test is whether the attorney's performance constitutes ineffective assistance. Here the attorney made no error.

United States v. Cronic, 466 U.S. 648 (1984)

90. Lineup

Yes. The constitutional right to counsel (Sixth Amendment) attaches (applies) at each "critical stage" of a criminal case. A lineup after one is formally charged with a crime is a critical stage. A lineup prior to arrest or formal charge is not a critical stage.

United States v. Wade, 388 U.S. 218 (1967)

91. Plain View

Yes. If police are conducting a lawful search or are otherwise on premises lawfully, they may seize evidence in plain view, even if the warrant does not cover that evidence. Before this case, the plain-view doctrine applied only where an officer inadvertently came upon evidence (as opposed to during a deliberate search).

Horton v. California, 496 U.S. 128 (1990)

92. Reverse Discrimination

Yes. Title VII of the United States Civil Rights Act of 1964 prohibits different treatment of employees based solely on race (white as well as nonwhite).

McDonald v. Santa Fe Trail Transportation Co., 427 U.S. 273 (1976)

93. Discriminating Effect

No. A law can be specifically designed such that it would have a discriminatory effect without the presence of "discriminatory intent." This law was

enacted not to keep women out of jobs, but to help military veterans get jobs. A female military veteran would also get the benefit of the law if she applied.
Personnel Administrator of Massachusetts v. Feeney, 422 U.S. 256 (1979)

94. Fertile Grounds
No. Sex discrimination is allowed only where there is a "bona fide occupational qualification" reasonably necessary to the normal operation of a business. Here, being fertile does not interfere with job performance. Therefore, Dumco can comply with safety standards and inform employees of potential hazards to limit its liability rather than prohibit "fertile" employees from performing certain jobs.
International Union, UAW v. Johnson Controls, Inc., 499 U.S. 187 (1991)

95. Affirmative Action
Yes. Title VII does not allow an employer to discriminate against some employees on the basis of race just because it has a process to benefit other employees of the same race. Title VII is designed to protect individuals, not just classes of people.
Connecticut v. Teal, 457 U.S. 440 (1992)

96. Uninvited Pest
No. Whether a person would pose for nude photos outside of work is immaterial to whether she would find conduct such as Ollie's "offensive." In this case,

the lower court reasoned erroneously that a person who would pose nude for a magazine would not be offended by Ollie's conduct.

Burns v. McGregor Electronic Industries, 989 F.2d 959 (8th Cir. 1993)

97. Legal Discrimination

No. Employment decisions can be based on a person's accent if the accent would materially interfere with job performance. Here the discrimination was not based solely on national origin—the employer had a legitimate reason not to hire Frank.

Fragante v. City and County of Honolulu, 888 F.2d. 591 (9th Cir. 1989)

98. Qualified Individuals

No. Professional schools may impose physical qualifications for admission if the qualifications are required to perform essential functions of the profession. Federal law does not prohibit discrimination against all handicapped people—only those who are "qualified individuals with a disability." Here, Maggie was actually not qualified because of the disability.

Southeastern Community College v. Davis, 442 U.S. 397 (1979)

99. Labor Dispute

No. An employer can fire an employee for cause for attacking the quality of the employer's goods or services (disloyalty), even if this attack takes place during a labor dispute.

NLRB v. Local 1229, IBEW (Jefferson Standard Broadcasting Co.), 346 U.S. 464 (1953)

100. Accommodations

No. An employer has a duty to make *reasonable* accommodation for persons with disabilities. This means doing what is necessary to allow the disabled worker to work in reasonable comfort. Conditions do not have to be identical for disabled and nondisabled workers. Here the agency made sufficient accommodations to satisfy the law.

Vande Zande v. State of Wisconsin Department of Administration, 44 F3d. 538 (7th Cir. 1995)

101. Union Rules

Yes. An elected union official can't be fired for opposing union rules. This action interferes with union members' right to elect. If Lonnie had been "appointed" by union leaders rather than elected by members, it would have been different. Also, the court believed that such a "chilling" of speech in the context of union activity was unacceptable.

Sheet Metal Workers' Int'l Association v. Lynn, 488 U.S. 347 (1989)

102. Marriage License

Yes. Where a state intends that failure to obtain a state marriage license will make the marriage void, the state usually specifies this in the law. Otherwise, the marriage is valid, but the failure to have the required license is sufficient grounds for dissolution.
Carabetta v. Carabetta, 438 A.2d 109 (1980)

103. Husbands' Rights

Yes. Paul erroneously argued that because he was still Jane's husband, he had a right to enter her apartment and, therefore, he could not be guilty of burglary (which is unlawful entry with intent to commit a crime). However, Jane had sole ownership of the property, so Paul had no right to be there.
Cladd v. State, 398 So. 2d 442 (1981)

104. Split the Baby

A: Yes. B: Yes.

The marriage is void because Alan could not have a valid marriage to Debbie, being already married to Janet. However, Debbie, being a "putative" wife (believing in good faith she is in a valid marriage), is entitled to inherit her fair share. Here Debbie received half.
In re Estate of Vargas, 36 Cal. App. 3d 714 (1974)

105. Marital Property

No. The general rule is that gifts are excluded from marital property. However, if the gift giver did not intend the items to be gifts, then the items would be included in marital property. There was evidence here that these were not purchased and given as gifts, but as investments.

O'Neill v. O'Neill, 600 S.W.2d 493 (1980)

106. Parents' Right

A: Yes. B: Yes.

Under the U.S. Constitution, parents have a right to direct the upbringing and education of their children—in particular their religious upbringing. However, states may enact and enforce compulsory school laws to ensure that children are given an opportunity to become productive members of society and not be harmed by, for example, being forced to work at a young age. Here the compulsory school law was constitutional, but, as applied to Jonas and Wally, it was not. The court held that compulsory education was not more important than the parents' right to free exercise of religion, on their own and on their children's behalf. The Court found no evidence that the children were being harmed by not having what amounted to two additional years of state-compelled education. It is important to note that constitutional rights such as free exercise of religion belong not only to adults, but to minors as well. Here, the Court did not address the children's wishes, since there had been no evidence that the children had expressed any different desire from that of their parents. The Court viewed this case as involving only parents' rights. Wisconsin v. Yoder, 406 U.S. 205 (1972)

107. Family Ties

No. Biological fathers do not have an unfettered right to notice of a pending adoption in all cases. The Due Process Clause and Equal Protection Clause of the U.S. Constitution do generally protect a parent's right to have a relationship with his or her child. However, the Supreme Court has recognized that where a parent has done nothing to build a relationship with the child, the child's interest in being adopted may be greater. In this case, Johnny had rarely seen the child, provided no financial support, and had not even taken the steps to assert his right as the father by registering to be notified. Lehr v. Robertson et al., 463 U.S. 248 (1983)

PLAYING
WITH OTHERS

Reading this book alone and testing your-self to see whether you have a finely tuned legal mind is fun and challenging, but competing with others always adds an extra thrill (especially if you win!).

Playing with Two
Simply take turns reading the cases and guessing the verdicts, writing down each guess on a score sheet before reading the answer. Each player gets one point for each correct answer and one point for each incorrect answer of the other player. The play-er with the most points wins.

Example: Player A and player B each guess the verdict correctly. Each player gets one point. If player A guesses correctly and player B guesses incorrectly, player A gets two points.

Playing with Three
One player is the judge. The other two players are attorneys. The judge reads the case. The attorneys guess the verdict, writing each one on a score sheet before the verdict is read. If neither attorney guesses the verdict correctly, the judge gets two Verdict Points. If one attorney guesses correctly and the

other guesses incorrectly, the judge gets one Verdict Point and the attorney who guessed correctly gets one Verdict Point. If each attorney guesses correctly, they each get one Verdict Point and the judge gets none.

In addition, after the verdict is read, if an attorney who has correctly guessed the verdict can state the rationale, that attorney gets a Rationale Point. The judge determines whether the Rationale Point will be given for the rationale stated by the attorney. Where both attorneys get a correct answer and state the rationale, the judge decides who has made the better case; only one attorney may get the Rationale Point. If, in the judge's honest opinion, neither player states the rationale correctly, the judge gets the Rationale Point. If neither attorney guesses the verdict correctly, the judge, in addition to getting the two Verdict Points, also gets the Rationale Point.

For each case, there are a total of three points to be earned (two Verdict Points and one Rationale Point). The player with the most points wins. To make sure judgment is impartial, the players must switch roles so that each has a chance to play the judge after one-third and then two-thirds of the cases have been read.

Examples: Attorney A and Attorney B each guess the verdict correctly. Then each attorney states the rationale, and the judge determines that Attorney A stated the rationale more accurately. Attorney A will get one Verdict Point and one Rationale Point for a total of two points, Attorney B will get one Verdict Point, and the judge will get none.

Attorney A guesses the verdict correctly. Attorney B is incorrect. Attorney A states an incorrect rationale. Attorney A will get one Verdict Point, Attorney B will get none, and the judge will get one Verdict Point and one Rationale Point for a total of two points.

If Attorney A and Attorney B each state an incorrect verdict, the Judge will get three points (two Verdict Points and one Rationale Point).

Index

Pages in **bold** refer to Holdings. Numbers in *italics* refer to case #.